ALL ABOUT

Sound

ANNA CLAYBOURNE

raintree
a Capstone company — publishers for children

Raintree is an imprint of Capstone Global Library Limited, a company incorporated in England and Wales having its registered office at 264 Banbury Road, Oxford, OX2 7DY – Registered company number: 6695582

www.raintree.co.uk
myorders@raintree.co.uk

Originated by Capstone Global Library Ltd
Printed and bound in India

ISBN 978 1 4747 7723 0 (hardback)
ISBN 978 1 4747 7729 2 (paperback)

British Library Cataloguing in Publication Data
A full catalogue record for this book is available from the British Library.

Acknowledgements
We would like to thank the following for permission to reproduce photographs:
Cover: Shutterstock: Leigh Prathe. Inside: Dreamstime: Fernando Gregory 43; Shutterstock: AAresTT 11, AISPIX by Image Source 31, Anyamuse 30, Anton Balazh 26-27, Samuel Borges Photography 5r, 45, Suede Chen 33, Lucie Danninger 27b, Deepspace 41, Goran Djukanovic 25, Ivica Drusany 17, ESB Professional 19, Everett Collection 38, Julie Ten Eyck 29, Eric Fahrner 40, Mika Heittola 34, Chris Howey 21, Brian A Jackson 44, Bryant Jayme 6, DG Jervis 16, Lucky Business 42, Majesticca 9, Steve Mann 8, Gino Santa Maria 1, 10, Matauw 32, Maxstockphoto 4, Monkey Business Images 36, Vladimir Mucibabic 35, Natursports 3, 18, Christopher Parypa 15, Pavel L Photo and Video 23, PavelShynkarou 20, Ondrej Penicka 5b, Jose AS Reyes 7, 45, Rob Stark 28, Ronald Sumners 13, Nicholas Sutcliffe 24, Tom Wang 14, Wavebreakmedia 22, Piotr Wawrzyniuk 39, Andrey Yurlov 12; Wikimedia Commons: Levin C. Handy 37.

Every effort has been made to contact copyright holders of material reproduced in this book. Any omissions will be rectified in subsequent printings if notice is given to the publisher.

All the internet addresses (URLs) given in this book were valid at the time of going to press. However, due to the dynamic nature of the internet, some addresses may have changed, or sites may have changed or ceased to exist since publication. While the author and publisher regret any inconvenience this may cause readers, no responsibility for any such changes can be accepted by either the author or the publisher.

Contents

What is sound?

We all know what sounds are. Footsteps, banging doors, talking, music, the noisy traffic on the road outside and the wind whooshing through the trees – these are all examples of sounds that we hear. Do you know how sounds happen?

 A huge crowd of people clapping and cheering makes a very loud sound!

Sound and movement

All sounds are made by something moving. Think of clapping your hands, scribbling with a pencil or switching on a noisy fan or vacuum cleaner. When things like this happen, the movements make objects vibrate (shake back and forth) very quickly. We can detect these vibrations using our ears – and that is what sounds are.

Different sounds

Sounds can be very different from each other. Some are loud and some are quiet, some are high and squealing, some low and rumbling. Different objects, materials and actions all make their own noises.

Hidden clues

Sounds can give us clues about what is happening around us. We also use sound when we talk, which is one of the main ways that humans communicate. In human speech alone, there are hundreds of different possible sounds. In the world as a whole, there are millions of different sounds.

Using technology such as mobile phones, we can now use sound to talk to anyone, anywhere in the world.

LIFE WITHOUT SOUND

Can you imagine life in total silence? It is very rare to experience this because there is almost always something you can hear. Even if you are deaf, you are likely to hear ringing or buzzing sounds in your head, and many deaf people can hear a little using a hearing aid. Scientists have found that being in total silence makes most people feel nervous.

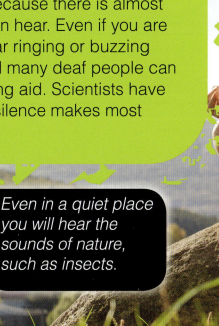

Even in a quiet place you will hear the sounds of nature, such as insects.

Chapter One

Sound all around

What can you hear right now? Perhaps it is the sound of a radio, a dog barking nearby, a passing car or people chatting all around you. Even when you are working or reading, you can hear your own breathing, the rustling of pages, the hum of a computer or the tapping of a keyboard.

Ambulance sirens are designed to be loud and piercing, to cut through the sounds of normal traffic.

Helpful sounds

We are used to being surrounded by sounds, even at times we think of as quiet and peaceful. There are many sounds we would find it hard to live without. When your microwaved food is ready, the microwave oven goes "ding" or "beep". A school bell tells you when it is home time, and your doorbell tells you that your friends have arrived. Ambulances and fire engines use their sirens to warn everyone that they are approaching at high speed, helping us all to stay safe.

Sounds for fun

As well as being useful, sounds can make us happy – especially musical sounds. Most of us hear music every day, on the radio, on television or from music players. Music can help people relax, dance and even concentrate. People use music to create the right mood in films, and to celebrate special occasions such as weddings and birthdays.

The sound of your favourite music can make you happy, calm you or make you want to dance!

SUPER SCIENCE FACT

The less sound there is around you, the higher your brain "turns up the volume" inside your head. So when it is very quiet, you pay attention to noises you normally would not notice, such as rustling leaves or a creaky floorboard.

Stop that noise!

There are some sounds that are not pleasant to listen to, such as screaming, low-flying aircraft or loud music when you are trying to sleep. When sound is upsetting or annoying, we are more likely to call it noise.

Sound pollution

Pollution means something damaging that escapes into our surroundings. It is usually used to talk about things such as waste chemicals. Unwanted noise can also be a type of pollution if it causes problems for people. For example, you might suffer from sound pollution if you live or work near an airport where aircraft noise can make it hard to sleep or concentrate. Very loud music, factory and traffic noise, and animal noises can also cause sound pollution.

The people who live in this house have to listen to an ear-splitting noise every time a plane takes off or lands.

Sounds in the sea

Sound pollution is also sometimes harmful to animals, especially sea creatures. Noises from ships' engines and undersea mining can interfere with the sounds animals such as dolphins use to communicate and find their way (see page 27).

The squeaky sound of chalk writing on a board is a noise that many people find unbearable.

Nasty noises

Why do we find some noises so horrible? Scientists think that noises linked to illness, such as the sound of vomiting, are upsetting because they make us think of germs that we want to avoid. Some noises are horrible simply because they are so loud that they are painful to listen to and can damage our ears. However, no one knows why people hate certain harmless noises, such as the screeching sounds of chair legs scraping on the floor or a fork sliding across a plate.

SUPER SCIENCE FACT

Scientists have found that children who go to school somewhere quiet find it easier to learn, read and concentrate than those whose school is in a noisy place.

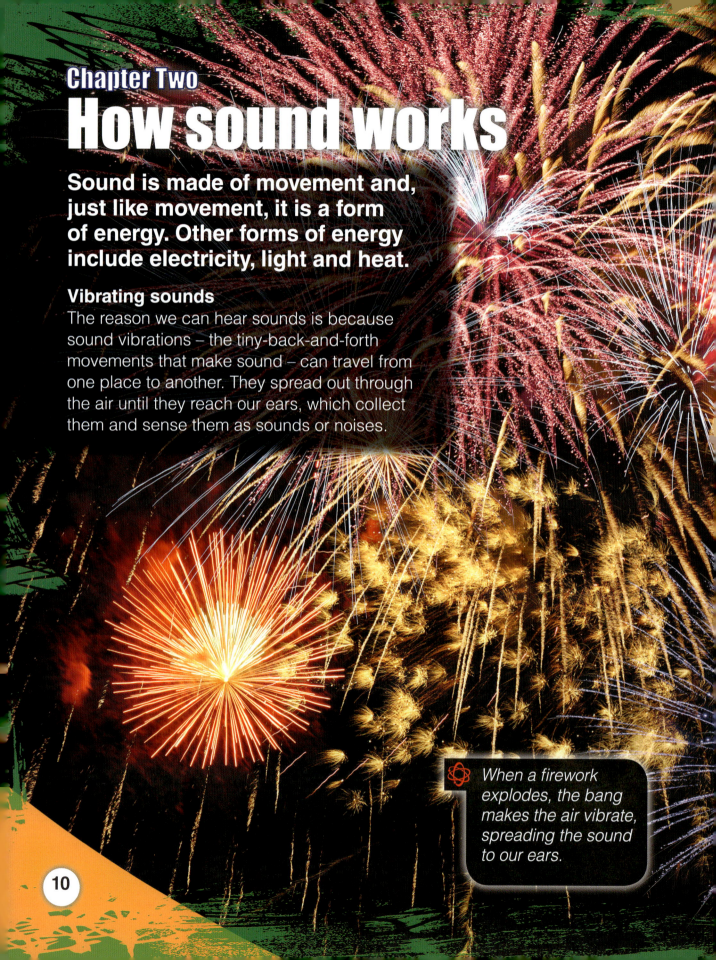

Chapter Two
How sound works

Sound is made of movement and, just like movement, it is a form of energy. Other forms of energy include electricity, light and heat.

Vibrating sounds

The reason we can hear sounds is because sound vibrations – the tiny-back-and-forth movements that make sound – can travel from one place to another. They spread out through the air until they reach our ears, which collect them and sense them as sounds or noises.

When a firework explodes, the bang makes the air vibrate, spreading the sound to our ears.

Playing drums sets off many patterns of sound vibrations, making a clattering, bashing noise.

How does sound travel?

Imagine something that is making a sound, like a bell ringing. It may be some distance away, but you know it is ringing because its vibrations reach your ears. This is what happens: the bell rings when its clapper (the part inside that swings back and forth) hits the bell, making the whole bell vibrate. As the bell vibrates, it pushes against the air around it, and the air starts to vibrate, too. The vibrations spread out through the air, going in every direction. If people are nearby, the vibrations enter their ears and they hear the sound.

Other sounds

The same thing happens with all sounds. When you speak, bands of muscle in your throat, called vocal cords, vibrate and pass their vibrations into the air. A guitar string or an elastic band vibrates when you pluck it, and the skin of a drum vibrates when you hit it.

SUPER SCIENCE FACT

To make a sound, another form of energy has to be converted into sound energy. For example, you use kinetic (movement) energy, to hit a drum, and this energy is converted into sound energy.

Sound waves

Sound travels in tiny, repeated patterns called sound waves. You cannot see them in the air because air is invisible.

Just like sound waves, a wave on the sea travels forward, carrying energy with it.

What are waves?

Think of ocean waves. The waves are movements of the water that travel from one place to another across the water's surface. However, the water itself does not move far – it just bobs up and down as the wave passes.

Sound waves

Sound waves are similar to ocean waves. They do the same thing, but instead of moving across a surface, they spread out in every direction. Instead of making the air move up and down, they make it move back and forth.

SUPER SCIENCE FACT

Sometimes you can even feel very loud sounds "thumping" into you as the sound waves travelling through the air hit your body.

How does it work?

Air and other substances are made up of tiny parts called molecules. When an object vibrates, it makes the molecules around it vibrate, too, and this creates sound waves. For example, as a bell vibrates back and forth, it pushes against the air molecules that are closest to it. These molecules move forward a little, and push against the molecules next to them. Molecules also move, and push against the molecules next to them – and so on. As they shift forward, the molecules leave a space behind them. As they bump into the next molecules, they create a crowded area where the molecules are close together. The bands of empty and crowded air are sound waves.

13

The speed of sound

Sound travels very fast! The speed of sound in air is around 1,200 kilometres (770 miles) per hour. It takes sound just under five seconds to travel 1.6 kilometres (1 mile), and 0.01 seconds to zoom across a room. Sound travels so quickly that you usually do not notice the time it takes to reach you.

SUPER SCIENCE FACT

You can sometimes tell that sound takes a while to reach you. Sound travels much more slowly than light. If you see something noisy happening a long way off, you might not hear the sound until a little while later. For example, at a baseball game, you might see the batter hit the ball – then hear the "clonk!" around a second later.

If you were this close to a baseball bat, you would hear it hit the ball almost straight away. From the back of the stadium, you would hear it a little while later.

This F-15 can fly at speeds of up to 2.5 times the speed of sound!

Supersonic!

Some aircraft and cars are "supersonic". This means that they can travel faster than the speed of sound or "break the sound barrier". The speed of sound in air is also known as Mach 1. If an aircraft flies at Mach 2, it is flying at twice the speed of sound. Some super high-speed, rocket-powered planes can travel as fast as Mach 6 (that is six times the speed of sound).

Sonic boom

When a vehicle such as a jet plane breaks the sound barrier, it makes a loud booming noise called a sonic boom. This is because at the speed of sound, the sound waves coming forward from the plane cannot escape, as the plane is travelling at the same speed as them. Instead, they pile up together, creating an extra-powerful sound wave – the boom.

High and low

When you hear someone playing a musical instrument or singing a tune, you can hear the notes going up and down. How high or low a sound is, is called pitch.

A tiger's growl is one of the lowest-pitched animal noises.

Squeaks and growls

All sounds have pitch. A mouse squeaking is a very high-pitched sound, and a tiger growling is a very low-pitched sound. An emergency siren whoops up and down, from high-pitched to low-pitched and back again. The pitch of our voices also rises and falls whenever we talk.

What causes pitch?

Pitch is decided by how fast an object and the molecules in the air around it are vibrating back and forth. The faster they vibrate, the higher the pitch. Small objects, or strings that are very short or tightly stretched, vibrate faster and make a higher-pitched sound than big or long objects. For example, a big, heavy bell vibrates slowly, and makes a low "DONG!" sound, while a tiny bell vibrates very fast, making a high-pitched, tinkling sound.

Famous singer José Carreras is a tenor, meaning he sings in a fairly high-pitched male voice.

Measuring pitch

Pitch is measured in vibrations per second, or Hertz (Hz). If you press the middle C key on a piano, the note you hear is around 262 Hz. A young child's voice can be as high as 400 Hz. Even low-pitched sounds vibrate many times per second. A very deep male voice, for example, is around 70 Hz.

LIFE WITHOUT INTONATION

The changing pitch of our voices is called intonation. We use it all the time to add meaning and emotion to what we say. To see how important pitch is, try speaking to someone without changing the pitch of your voice at all.

How loud?

When you want the television to be a bit louder, you turn up the volume. But what exactly is happening to the sound when you do that? Whether a sound is loud or quiet is decided by how much energy it is carrying. In loud sound waves, the molecules have more kinetic energy, and move a bigger distance back and forth, than they do in quiet sound waves.

Racing motorcycles make a deafening noise as they zoom around the track at top speed.

Big vibrations

The size of the back-and-forth movement in a sound wave is called amplitude. When you increase the amplitude of a sound, you put in more energy, and make the sound louder. For example, if you hit a drum gently, you put only a little energy into it. The drum skin vibrates only a small distance back and forth, and so do the air molecules around it, making low-amplitude sound waves. If you want a bigger, louder bang, you hit the drum really hard, using more energy. This makes bigger vibrations and high-amplitude sound waves.

Deafening decibels

We use a system called the decibel (dB) scale to measure how loud things sound. Zero on the scale is the quietest sound humans can possibly hear. The loudest sounds ever heard, such as huge volcanic eruptions, are thought to reach as high as 190 dB.

If you were working quietly in a library, the sound around you would measure around 30 decibels.

SUPER SCIENCE FACT

The world's loudest animal is thought to be the blue whale, which is also the biggest animal. Its calls have been measured at a staggering 188 dB.

Chapter Three
Sound effects

Sound can bounce, change direction and travel amazingly long distances. We can also do lots of things to sound to control it, change it and make it louder or quieter.

Sound reflections

If you were blindfolded and led into a room you had never been in before, you could probably tell a lot about it just from the sound. It might sound big or small, cosy and welcoming, or hard and empty. We can tell these things from the way sound reflects (bounces off) different surfaces.

Echoes

An echo happens when sound reflects off a surface and returns to where it started. For example, if you stand opposite a cliff face and shout loudly, you may hear your shout echoing. To hear a true, clear echo, you have to be standing at least 12 metres (40 feet) away from the surface, so that the shout and its echo do not merge together.

An empty room sounds different from a fully furnished room, because of the echoes.

Reverberation

A large, empty room with bare walls and floors can sound "echoey". However, when echoes all blend together as they do inside a room, it is called reverberation, rather than being a true echo. Soft surfaces, such as carpets, soak up sound instead of reflecting it, and they reduce reverberation.

In 2012, the world-famous Sydney Opera House had new ceiling panels fitted to improve its acoustics.

Sound control

Sometimes we want to make sound louder (amplify it) so that everyone can hear a speech or concert. Sometimes we want to muffle it, to make sure loud noises, such as a band rehearsing, do not bother people nearby.

Turn it up!

One way to make yourself sound louder is to speak through a megaphone – a hollow cone with holes at both ends. Megaphones trap the sound waves coming from your mouth and direct them forwards so that the people in front of you hear a louder sound. Without a megaphone, the sound waves would shoot off in all directions.

A megaphone is useful for speaking to a crowd of people – but this close, it would be far too loud!

Electric sound

We can also make sound louder by adding energy to it in the form of electricity. This is how electric megaphones and public-address systems work. A microphone picks up the sound and turns it into an electrical signal. An amplifier makes the signal stronger, and a speaker then turns it back into sound waves by making a cone vibrate.

The carpeted walls in this rehearsal room help to stop the sound escaping.

Turn it down!

Muffling and making sound quieter is called soundproofing. To soundproof a room, it can be lined with a material that absorbs or soaks up sound, instead of reflecting it or letting it through. Soft and squishy materials, such as foam, rubber and sponge, work best.

Musical instruments

Most musical instruments make sounds that can change up or down in pitch, so that they can play a tune – a pattern of notes. There are many different types of musical instrument, and different ways for them to change pitch.

Changing pitch

In stringed instruments, such as guitars and violins, tighter or shorter strings make higher-pitched sounds. Players use their fingers to change the length of the strings and to change the pitch. In wind instruments, the length of the tube decides the pitch. For example, covering the finger holes on a flute, or sticking out the slide on a trombone, makes the tube longer and the pitch lower. Some instruments have separate parts that have their own pitch, such as the keys of a xylophone.

The pitch of these instruments is changed by changing the length of the strings.

Adding rhythm

A few instruments, such as a tambourine and snare drum, have just one pitch that does not change. These instruments are usually used to mark the rhythm in a piece of music.

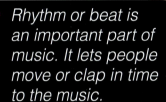

Rhythm or beat is an important part of music. It lets people move or clap in time to the music.

Changing volume

You make a sound louder by putting in more energy. With most instruments, you can make them louder by blowing, plucking or hitting harder. You can make them quieter by being more gentle.

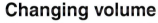

LIFE WITHOUT MUSIC

Can you imagine life without any music? Music is a huge part of our lives. With no music, there would be no songs on the radio or television, no sports anthems, ballets or pop bands. And without music, you would not be able to hum to yourself!

Sound and substances

In everyday life, we are used to sound waves zooming through the air to our ears. Sound can travel through other substances, too, including water and solid materials such as wood and glass.

Super-speedy sound

Sound travels faster and further in liquids and solids than it does in air. This is because liquids and solids contain more molecules, and the molecules are closer together. It is easier for them to bump against each other, and allow sound waves to travel.

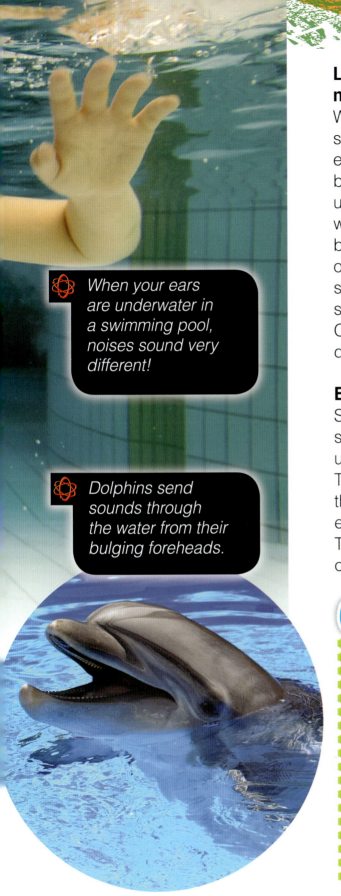

When your ears are underwater in a swimming pool, noises sound very different!

Dolphins send sounds through the water from their bulging foreheads.

Long-distance messages

Whales and some other sea creatures can "talk" to each other over great distances by calling or singing to each other underwater. Scientists think that a blue whale's song, for example, can be heard by another blue whale that is thousands of kilometres away. Elephants do something similar on land. They make sounds that make the ground vibrate. Other elephants many kilometres away detect the vibrations through their feet.

Echolocation

Some animals, such as dolphins, use sound echoes as a way of finding things underwater. This is called echolocation. The dolphin beams a high-pitched noise through the water, then detects the echoes that bounce off nearby objects. This gives the dolphin a clear "picture" of what is around it, even in the dark.

SUPER SCIENCE FACT

Humans use a form of echolocation called sonar. A sonar system on a ship sends out sounds, then collects the echoes that bounce back from the seabed. The time the echoes take to return shows how deep the sea is. Sonar systems can also reveal underwater objects such as submarines and shoals of fish.

Chapter Four

Sensing sounds

As sound is all around us, it makes sense that humans, as well as most other animals, have ears that let us hear it and make use of it.

Being able to speak and listen means we can communicate all types of information, ideas and thoughts to each other.

LIFE WITHOUT PINNAS

If you did not have your pinnas, hearing would be much harder. Your ears would not collect as much sound, and it would be easier for sweat, rain and dirt to get into your ears and block them.

About ears

Your two ears are positioned on the sides of your head, the best place for hearing sounds from as many directions as possible. The rounded, wrinkled-looking part of your ear that you can see is called the pinna or outer ear. Your ears actually have many other parts, too, but most of them are inside your head where you cannot see them.

Collecting vibrations

The shape of the outer ear is very important. It catches sound waves and directs them into the middle of the ear, where they move down a tube called the ear canal. At the end of the ear canal is a thin, tightly stretched sheet called the eardrum. When sound waves push against the eardrum, they make it vibrate.

Going in!

The eardrum then passes the vibrations on through three tiny bones, and into a snail-shaped ear part called the cochlea. By now, the vibrations are deep inside your head. Your cochleas are just behind your eyeballs.

What do your pinnas look like? Everyone's ears have a unique shape.

Sound and the brain

Sound is patterns of sound waves, some louder and faster than others, crashing into your ears. So how do you experience this inside your head as the sound of music, a coin you dropped hitting the floor or your mum shouting?

Into the brain

The cochlea, deep inside the ear, is where sound vibrations are sent to the brain. Tiny hairs in the cochlea pick up the vibrations and turn them into electrical signals. They travel along pathways called nerves to the parts of the brain that deal with sound.

You can recognize a rooster's "cock-a-doodle-do!" because your brain has heard it before, and stored a memory of it.

Making sense of sound

When the brain receives a sound signal, it compares the patterns in it to other sounds stored in its memory. This is how you can recognize names, tunes or sounds such as running water, a dog's bark and a car engine.

When you are busy reading, you can be "in your own world", because your brain tunes out the sounds around you.

Parts of the brain

We have special brain areas for making sense of different types of sound. A brain part called the auditory cortex, just above the ear, processes sounds such as music, and links the patterns to memories. Wernicke's area, a part towards the back of the brain behind your ears, deals with speech, separating out words and working out what sentences mean.

Animal ears

Some animals have more sensitive hearing than humans. These animals can detect sounds that are too high-pitched for people to hear. Other animals can sense sounds even though they have no ears at all!

Big ears!

Some animals have developed enormous ears to help them hear. The fennec fox's ears, for example, are almost as big as its head. The fox's sharp hearing helps it to catch prey that burrows underground.

Hares have huge ears to listen out for predators such as wolves and big cats.

The best listeners

Animals such as dolphins, cats, bats, rats and owls all have super-sensitive hearing. Dolphins and bats can hear much higher-pitched sounds than we can. Porpoises can hear higher sounds than any other animal – as high as 150,000 Hertz.

Owl ears

Owls have extremely sensitive hearing. This helps them to track down mice and other small prey. Owls' ears are covered by feathers. They have no pinnas to collect sound waves. Instead, the large, dish-shaped circles around an owl's eyes do this job. They catch sound and funnel it towards the owl's ear holes.

No ears!

Many small animals, such as insects and snails, have no ears. Snails detect sound vibrations through the ground, and through the air using their tentacles. Grasshoppers can hear each other chirping using their tympani, which work like eardrums. Instead of being on the grasshopper's head, they are on its knees or the sides of its body.

This grasshopper's tympani are little ovals on its sides, just in front of its back legs.

SUPER SCIENCE FACT

Dolphins have amazingly good hearing, but their ears are just tiny holes. They pick up sound vibrations in the water, mainly through their jawbones.

Living with deafness

If you have good hearing, it is hard to imagine how you would cope without the information your ears are giving you all the time. There are, however, many ways to get around the lack of sound.

Modern technology is very helpful if you are deaf – it is easy to send a text message or email instead of talking on the phone.

What causes deafness?

Some people are born deaf because some of the body parts needed for hearing, such as the hairs inside the cochlea, are missing or do not work properly. There are also some illnesses, such as measles, that can damage the ears and cause deafness. Most people also begin to lose their sense of hearing as they get older. As people age, the hairs inside the cochlea start to weaken and work less well.

Hearing aids

People who struggle to hear, but are not completely deaf, can use hearing aids to help them hear better. Hearing aids are like small, battery-powered megaphones that sit behind or in the ear. They pick up sounds, amplify them and play them loudly into the ear.

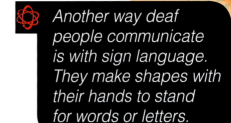

Another way deaf people communicate is with sign language. They make shapes with their hands to stand for words or letters.

Cochlear implant

Some people who are severely deaf can have a device, called a cochlear implant, transplanted into their ear to do the job of the cochlea. The implant picks up sounds and turns them into signals, which it sends along nerves to the brain.

SUPER SCIENCE FACT

As well as using our ears, humans can often sense sound vibrations through touch. If you press a balloon against a stereo speaker, you may feel it vibrating as the sound waves pass through it. The famous composer Beethoven went deaf, but sensed sound vibrations through his skull by pressing a stick against his piano with his forehead.

Chapter Five
Sound machines

In the last few hundred years, there have been all kinds of amazing inventions that have allowed us to use sound in new ways.

Recorded sounds make computer games much more exciting!

Recording sound

Sound recording means capturing a sound and storing it so that it can be played back. Because of this, we can listen to music on CDs and media players, hear speech and action in films and television programmes or pick up a recorded telephone message.

How it all began

In the 1800s, inventors found that sound vibrations in the air could make a thin, tightly stretched diaphragm, similar to an eardrum, vibrate. By attaching a needle to the diaphragm, its movements could be used to scratch a pattern on a moving surface. This was like a written record of the sound, but it could not be played back.

The phonograph

In 1877, Thomas Edison built a machine, called a phonograph, which could record and play back sound. As a sound was made, the phonograph picked up the vibrations and scratched a pattern in a rotating, foil-covered cylinder. Running the needle through the scratch again made the diaphragm vibrate, playing back the same sound.

Thomas Edison poses with an early version of his phonograph, one of his many inventions.

LIFE WITHOUT RECORDINGS

What was it like when there were no sound recordings? Long ago, bands of musicians travelled around, playing music for anyone who would pay them. At parties, people took turns to play instruments such as the lute, harpsichord or piano. Being able to play an instrument made you very popular: *you* were the entertainment!

Long-distance sounds

When you turn on the radio, you can hear someone talking to you from hundreds of kilometres away. And if you want to chat to a friend on the other side of the world, you can, by using a telephone or computer!

In the early days of telephones, operators had to connect each call using wires.

Telephones

Today, we use mainly mobile phones and cordless handsets, but the first telephones worked using wires. In the 1830s, scientists invented the telegraph, a way of sending messages along wires as patterns of electrical signals. The telephone added to this by using a diaphragm at each end of the wire. One diaphragm captured voice sounds and turned them into electrical signals. The other turned the signals at the other end of the wire back into movements and sound waves.

LIFE WITHOUT MOBILE PHONES

Today, many people have mobile phones, but 30 years ago, mobile phones were very rare and mainly seen in sci-fi films. If you went out to meet a friend, you had to plan a meeting place and time first. If they were not there, bad luck! If you got stuck in traffic or lost on a mountainside, you could not call or text anyone. Mobile phones have truly changed our lives.

Tune in!

Radio waves are a kind of electromagnetic wave that can travel across empty space. James Clerk Maxwell discovered how these waves worked in the 1860s. In the 1890s, scientists worked out how to make changes to the size and shape of radio waves, so that they could carry patterns such as sound-wave patterns. A radio set collects the wave signal and turns these patterns back into sounds.

Today, many people use their mobile phones not only to keep in touch, but also to play music.

Ultrasound and infrasound

Ultrasound means sound that is too high-pitched for humans to hear. Infrasound is sound that is too low-pitched for us to hear. Although we cannot hear them, both these types of sound are important, and both can be very useful.

An ultrasound scan of a baby before birth can show whether it is healthy and growing well.

Amazing ultrasound

Ultrasound has many amazing uses. A beam of ultrasound can work as a kind of sonar for looking inside the body. It bounces off organs and other body parts to create an image called an ultrasound scan. High-energy (or "loud" if we could hear it) ultrasound is wonderful for killing germs and dislodging dirt, so it is used for cleaning scientific tools and instruments, tiny machine parts and even teeth.

Some animals are extremely good at sensing infrasound. This may help to explain reports of animals becoming nervous or running away before an earthquake strikes.

If people could sense infrasound in the way some animals do, we might be able to avoid earthquakes and other natural disasters.

Infrasound rumbles

Although infrasound is too low for us to hear, we can sometimes sense it shaking our bodies. In fact, very loud infrasound can be dangerous, making people ill and damaging organs. It can also be useful. Volcanic and earthquake activity under the ground can create infrasound waves before an earthquake or eruption begins. If we can detect the sound using machines, it can act as an early warning system.

The bloop!

In 1997, an incredibly loud, low-pitched sound was recorded in the Pacific Ocean. For years, no one knew what it was, and many people thought this "bloop" might have come from a giant, unknown sea creature. Scientists now think it was probably made by icebergs breaking up.

Computer sounds

Computers can store and make changes to all types of information, including sounds. Computers store sounds as patterns of numbers.

Storage and playback

As computers can store a lot of information in their memory, they are a great place to keep recordings of music and other sounds. By connecting a computer to a speaker, you can play back the sounds. Smartphones and media players contain mini computers that do this, too, so you can carry all your music around with you wherever you go.

Over time, mobile phones and computers have become smaller and smaller, but they can hold more and more information, including music and videos.

Imagine the noise this flying saucer might make in an exciting sci-fi film. To create it, film-makers use computers and sound software.

Samples and synthesis

As well as storing songs, computers are used to record and store samples: snippets of sound made by musical instruments, voices, animals and any other sound you can think of. Musicians use computers to make changes to samples and put them together in patterns to make music. Computer-generated sounds are also used for film sound effects – for example, to create the sound of a spacecraft or a monster.

SUPER SCIENCE FACT

British physics professor Stephen Hawking had an illness that made it hard to move or talk, but he was able to communicate via speech synthesis. He used a computer to turn his words into speech so that he could talk to the people around him as well as give lectures and present television programmes.

Speech sounds

Today, you can pick up a smartphone and ask it a question, and it will talk back to you. Speech-recognition software can record your speech and make sense of it, convert it into text or follow your commands. Meanwhile, speech-synthesis software puts speech sounds together to make words, so that a computer can "speak" any sentence.

World of sound

Sound is incredibly important in our world. It is important to many inventions and machines, communications, and safety systems. Speech, music and natural sounds, such as waves on the beach, are good for people, too. They help us to relax and de-stress. Even if you cannot hear at all, you can benefit from sound, for example, by having an ultrasound scan or by using speech-recognition software.

We rely upon sound in almost everything we do, from hearing our alarm clocks ring in the morning to listening to relaxing music in the evening.

Sound of the future

Sound-related technology is moving faster than ever before, with new phones, recording devices and software appearing all the time. In the future, we will probably control hundreds of things by talking to them – from cars and wheelchairs to household appliances. New uses for ultrasound include bonding fabrics together to make clothes, and better ultrasound scans that could allow doctors to see inside the body to carry out surgery.

One day, the devices we use to listen to music may be so small that they are hardly detectable at all!

SUPER SCIENCE FACT

Sonar technology is used mainly in water over long distances, but newer versions, which work in the air, have been developed. They allow robots to "see" by detecting the things around them using echoes, so that they can avoid obstacles and pick up objects. There are also sonar wristbands and glasses that help blind people to sense nearby objects in the same way. As these improve, some people's sight could be mostly replaced by sound.

Smaller and smaller

As time goes on, we find ways to make smaller, better electronic parts, and electronic devices shrink. This will probably continue to happen, resulting in even tinier music storage devices, hearing aids and microphones.

45

Glossary

absorb soak up

amplifier device that adds energy to sound to make it louder

amplify make a sound louder

amplitude size of sound vibrations, depending on the amount of energy in a sound

cochlea snail-shaped part inside the ear

cochlear implant device fitted inside the ear that works like a cochlea to help people hear

diaphragm thin, tightly stretched skin used to pick up sound vibrations

ear canal passage leading into the ear

eardrum thin, tightly stretched sheet inside the ear that picks up sound vibrations

echo sound that has bounced off a surface and returned the way it came

echolocation method some animals use to sense their surroundings using echoes

electromagnetic wave type of wave energy that includes light, radio waves and X-rays

energy power to do work or make things happen

megaphone cone-shaped speaking device that makes speech sound louder

microphone device that collects sounds and turns them into electrical signals

molecules group of atoms that are bonded together

nerves pathways that carry signals between the brain and the rest of the body

outer ear part of the ear that you can see, also called the pinna

phonograph first sound recording and playback device

pinna part of the ear that you can see, also called the outer ear

predator animal that hunts and eats other animals

prey animals that are hunted and eaten by other animals

radio waves types of electromagnetic wave

reflect bounce off a surface

reverberation echoes that bounce off nearby surfaces and blend together

software sets of instructions used to make computers carry out particular jobs

sonar man-made system that uses echoes to measure distances and locate objects

sonic boom loud bang heard when a moving vehicle passes the speed of sound

soundproofing stopping sound from escaping

sound waves patterns of sound vibrations that move forward through a substance

speaker device that turns electrical signals into sounds by making vibrations

supersonic faster than the speed of sound

telegraph system for sending messages along wires in the form of electrical signals

tympani eardrum-like parts found on the bodies of some insects and other animals

ultrasound sound that is too high-pitched for humans to hear

ultrasound scan image of the inside of the body created using ultrasound echoes

vocal cords bands of muscle in the throat that vibrate to make voice sounds

Find out more

Books

100 Scientists Who Made History, Andrea Mills
(DK Children, 2018)

All About Physics (Big Questions), Richard Hammond
(DK Children, 2015)

From Crashing Waves to Music Download: An energy journey through the world of sound (Energy Journeys), Andrew Solway
(Raintree, 2016)

Light and Sound (Essential Physical Science),
Louise and Richard Spilsbury (Raintree, 2014)

Thomas Edison (Science Biographies), Kay Barnham
(Raintree, 2015)

Websites

www.bbc.com/bitesize/articles/zstr2nb
Learn more about how sounds are made.

www.dkfindout.com/uk/science/sound/using-sound-to-navigate
Find out how ships use sound to navigate, and take a sensational sound quiz!

Index